To Henry in Heaven

# To Henry in Heaven

*Reflections on the Loss of a Child*

Herbert Brokering

**Augsburg Books**

MINNEAPOLIS

To Lois Brokering,
whom some believe now rocks her grandson,
Henry Frederick Brokering, in heaven.

TO HENRY IN HEAVEN
Reflections on the Loss of a Child

Large-quantity purchases or custom editions of this book are available at a discount from the publisher. For more information, contact the sales department at Augsburg Fortress, Publishers, P.O. Box 1209, Minneapolis, MN 55440-1209.

*Library of Congress Cataloging-in-Publication Data*
Brokering, Herbert F.
To Henry in heaven : reflections on the loss of a child / Herbert Brokering.
  p. cm.
Includes bibliographical references.
ISBN 0-8066-5170-9 (pbk. : alk. paper)
1. Consolation. 2. Stillbirth—Religious aspects—Christianity—Meditations.
3. Miscarriage—Religious aspects—Christianity—Meditations. 4. Children—Death—
Religious aspects—Christianity—Meditations.  I. Title.
  BV4907.B77 2005
  242'.4--dc22          2004030182

Cover design by Laurie Ingram; cover photo © Gerrit Greve/CORBIS
Book design by Michelle L. N. Cook

The paper used in this publication meets the minimum requirements of American National Standard for Information Sciences—Permanence of Paper for Printed Library Materials, ANSI Z329.48-1985. ⊖ ™

Manufactured in the U.S.A.

09    08    07    06    05    1    2    3    4    5    6    7    8    9    10

# TABLE OF CONTENTS

# PREFACE

*To Henry in Heaven* is a collection of poems and spiritual dialogues between a grandfather and his stillborn grandchild, though the book's messages are meaningful to any family member experiencing the loss of an infant. In each of the imagined conversations, a loved one expresses thoughts and emotions of fear, want, loss, hurt, separation, loneliness, regret, blame, anger, and doubt. In the italicized reply, the child describes a higher life of peace, comfort, joy, light, wonder, trust, safety, and beauty. These dialogues demonstrate how family members can continue to talk intimately with the child who has died to make peace with this new life they have together.

I am seventy-eight years old. My grandson, Henry Frederick, lies under a maple.

H. L. B.

# OPENING LETTER

Dear God,

We are missing our first Christmas together. Our little one went straight from mother to heaven, one day before birth. He returned to you before we heard the birth-cry, before grasping our fingers, before nursing his mother. Our little one went to heaven before opening eyes to us, before saying daddy, before we did what we had prepared to do the next ten days, ten years, twenty, more.

How still our child came to us. Not a word, and we are filled with many unspoken words. All the years to come were done at his birth. In a single moment we saw all we had hoped to do. We held all the years and handed them with the child to each other.

Now what? Our hands are heavy with hope. All we planned on earth is finished. Everything that was to come has vanished.

Dear child, you have drawn us into God's holy place. We are full of wonder. We want to ask, do you see the angels? Do they know us? Is the river running? Do the choirs sound like choirs? Is a year long?

We held you at birth and heard the words "It is finished." Yet your life here is not finished. All we wished to do for you, to play with you, to sing to you . . . these are still our hopes. We hold our hopes in us, we feel them all, hear them like a love song.

All the words we would have said to you we still say, silently or softly spoken. All the places we would have gone with you we still go with you and more. We will climb hills with you though now we feel we can no longer climb. We will make tunes with you we cannot yet write. We will cry and run out of tears, and someday, we will laugh more deeply than we can now believe.

Little one, you have wakened life in us. You will take us to holy places. We will walk everywhere together. You will help us see sunsets that were hidden. You will call our attention to bird songs and human feelings and wind. We will hold your hand to go places we cannot go alone.

Dear God, a child in heaven leads us, sings to us, cheers us on. There is a host of heaven. We had planned to spend a Christmas together in our house. Now we celebrate in your house.

Dear God. Dear Henry.

Your Grandpa

*Poems and Conversations*

## You Know the Secrets

Dear God, you know the secrets
that always do unfold
and all the hidden stories
that still remain untold;

We do not ask for answers
so we can understand
but ask for our believing,
for death is in your hand.

We held our baby quiet
and cried so deep inside;
the earth seemed oh so darkened,
all worlds did collide.

Now in the still of seasons
that in our life unfold
bring peace into the spirit
of secrets still untold.

## Conversation: Leaving

What did you feel when you went?
> *You were there. We are connected.*

It happened unexpectedly.
> *I was told.*

By a voice?
> *A prediction.*

A warning?
> *A promise. I was given a promise.*

That all this would happen?
> *Of a journey. An unbelievable life.*

We planned for your journey.
> *What you planned is part of the promise.*

We waited, we hoped.
> *That is part of the journey, to hope.*

We prayed, we thanked.
> *To thank is part of the journey.*

We were choosing your name.
> *A soul needs a name for the journey.*

Did you feel when you left us?
> *I did not leave you. You have me with you. See, I am here.*

Were you startled?
> *In awe. I saw this light.*

Were you afraid?
> *All fear was swallowed by a song: Fear not.*

Did you cry?
> *My tears were wiped before they fell.*

Did you see us?
   *Through my tears being dried.*
Did this make you sad?
   *I am to be here.*
You are alright there.
   *I am here, and I am there.*
Are you sad?
   *The tears were wiped before they fell.*

# I Am Grieving

I am grieving.
Can you see
how I loved you inside me?

I am grieving.
Can you hear
how I want you to be near?

I am grieving
for your touch,
for I love you very much.

I am grieving.
Can you tell
when this grieving will be well?

I am grieving.
Can you feel
all I do to keep you real?

I am grieving.
Since you came
life will never be the same.

## CONVERSATION: STILLNESS

We held you. Stillborn is quiet. Once I thought you moved; I moved.

*I knew you held me.*

We did not want you to be so still.

*Death is not still.*

What is after death?

*Life.*

How much?

*There is no end to life.*

We wanted a lifetime with you the way we know life. A birth-cry, to hear your sucking, to see your toes flexing and your eyes squinting in the light. You were so still.

*You talked to me.*

As if you lived. In a few words we said so much.

*What did you say?*

Everything we would have said in ten or twenty years.

*What you thought I'd miss?*

And what we'd miss. We talked mostly about what we would miss.

*You are a good mother and a good father.*

We held you as though you'd live with us forever.

*I knew you held me.*

Our eyes never left you. We poured all our years into this little time, while we held you.

*Time can be full.*

We took all the years we wanted together and held them.

*Then?*

Then we let you go. We all did.
*Where did I go?*
Inside us. Where we can hold you. Where you will never leave.
You are a member of the family.
*You all held me.*
We kissed you and blessed you; we made holy signs on you.
*Now?*
There is no letting go.
*I will hold onto you.*
We will not let you go.
*Feel how I am holding onto you.*

## I Hold You

I held you
and in the tiny holding
it was I you held,
in silence.

I hold you
and still I need the holding;
it is I you hold,
in silence.

I hold you
and if you need the holding
it is you I hold,
in silence.

## Conversation: Holding You

I'm holding you the way we held you then.
  *In the room.*
The three of us, and the doctor.
  *I seemed quiet in your arms.*
My mind has stayed with you.
  *The way you saw me. You held me in the little room.*
Inside the hospital room with one window.
  *I was in your arms.*

I still hold you.

>*Now I can hold you, both of you.*

We listened for your breath.

>*I am breathing the warm wind. I feel your breath.*

You are breathing?

>*Souls have breath. Spirit is wind.*

Then you are moving.

>*We dance and run and swim and fly.*

You were strong. We said that.

>*I was on a great journey. Each soul must take the walk.*

You felt you were already walking?

>*We walk, we run, we fly, we swim.*

You swam in me.

>*And I danced and flew.*

You flew away so soon.

>*I took you with me. Beyond the little room.*

There are no walls?

>*I see no walls. I see us.*

Where do we go?

>*We go far inside each other.*

Where no one knows?

>*Where we know. You in me. I in you. We are one
>with each other.*

## A LIFETIME

We held you for a lifetime
in such a tiny room;
our hearts were overflowing
and then you left so soon,
but in this awesome hour
you opened wide a place
where saints and angels gather
in love and for embrace.
'Twas not of our own choosing,
we had another way
that baby would be with us
to walk through night and day;
that was another journey
we planned for years to come.
Oh how the years did hurry
inside that little room.


## CONVERSATION: BEING YOUR FATHER

You know I am your father.
> *Everyone gets a father. That's how it is.*

Your own real father.
> *Without you I would not be here. I owe myself to you.*

I meant you no harm. No pain. No hurt. No worry.
> *I have no pain or worry. I have a father and mother. So it is from the beginning.*

I know.

> *And always will be, as many say. Then they feel better.*

There are sayings that help. This conversation with you helps.

> *Talking with each other is what family does. We will always have conversation.*

You are so little.

> *I wasn't born yesterday. There are years in me. The ancestors.*

They are there. Those we did not know.

> *Now they are here. The ancestors and the descendants.*

That is a lot of people.

> *Souls. We count them as souls.*

You believe in souls?

> *I am one. That's where it begins and goes on.*

I am your father, and you are telling me all this.

> *We all know something that will help the other.*

I love you. I am your father. Yet we never ran or climbed or sang or played with teddy bears or had breakfast together.

> *You think about these things. You want them?*

I want all these things with you.

> *Then you are really my father. If you want these things then you are really my father.*

I am.

> *Stay my father. I will stay your child.*

## Is There a Time?

Is there a time when I will know
how deep and steep a valley
I can go?

Is there a time when I will see
how strong the strength of my soul is
inside me?

Is there a time when you will tell
how hurt and hope and weeping
make me well?

## Conversation: Picturing You

We often think of you as an angel.
*There are lots of ways for believers to imagine.*
You're so little but I can hear you talk.
*Everything we do is language. It's more than words.*
Sometimes I see you with wings. Invisible wings, but you can fly.
*There are surprises you have not yet seen.*
Angels, angels, angels. There seem to be so many. Do you feel
lost?
*There is a plan inside everything.*
You don't try to understand? Comprehend?
*We marvel. We are amazed. That is how spirit is.*
Your spirit is in us.
*Spirit will not go away.*
Do you wear a halo?
*Halo is not something to wear. It is always around us and
through us.*
Bright? White?
*All colors, at once. Colors not yet seen.*
Like decorations?
*We don't decorate. The beauty is always unfolding.*
How pretty?
*Inside out. More than eyes can see. More than ears can hear.*
Do angels know what to do?
*Angels don't need training. Spirit knows.*

# Felt You Dance

As mother and as father
we wished for you a birth;
we felt you dance inside us
to enter into earth.

Each day we felt your heart beat,
you danced with all your might,
we felt you in the morning
and often in the night.

Now dance with angels singing
around a heaven throne,
with us and those in heaven
where you are not alone.

You'll always be our baby
where saints and angels stay;
we know you are in heaven
and so we know the way.

## Conversation: The Lamb

We had a lamb for you.
    *The Lamb is here.*
A soft, wooly lamb for you to hug.
    *I know the Lamb.*
You could have taken the lamb to bed.
    *The Lamb is in our midst.*
You could have held the lamb, cuddled.
    *The Lamb and I hold each other.*
I want to hold you too.
    *Hold me.*


## Tonight

Tonight I let you hold me tight,
a sudden baby cry
and that is how you hold me right
in silence, then a sigh.

Tonight I feel you on my breast
and there we take our rest;
while sun and day set in the west
you hold me, I am blest,

Tonight I feel your baby touch,
you curl inside my lap
and there I love so very much,
your tiny baby touch.

## CONVERSATION: POURING OUT

He poured you like sand.
>    *My father.*
Your father said: Dust to dust.
>    *Many fathers and mothers must say these words.*
We are all from dust and return to dust.
>    *My father held me with his hands, then let go.*
Your father was on his knees pouring you into the earth.
>    *Earth to earth, ashes to ashes, dust to dust. It happens to us all.*
The ashes were in an envelope.
>    *A mother and father's letter. A love letter.*
Then I was not thinking of the ashes. I was thinking of who
you were.
>    *Who am I?*
More than the ashes. You are more.
>    *We are more than the ashes?*
Spirit. Body and spirit.
>    *He let me go from the envelope.*
Till the envelope was empty. Both were there, side by side.
Mother and father.
>    *They let me go.*
They laid you into the earth. Then covered you.
>    *Tucked me in. I am home.*
Where are you now?
>    *In the earth.*
Where they poured you out, they planted a tree.
>    *In the earth.*

It is winter. The leaves are gone. The ground is still.
*It will be spring. The leaves will bloom.*
They will come to visit the tree.
*And I will meet them there.*
At the tree?
*Wherever they pour me out, wherever they let me go.*
They did not throw you away.
*They held me and let me go; they poured me out.*
Can you feel them in the earth?
*The earth is a mother and a father. The earth embraced me
in their love.*
The tree is quiet.
*The tree will bloom.*

## Maple Tree

The maple tree is silent,
the snow upon each stem;
there is a sleep is so quiet
we know not why or when.

The maple tree is silent,
gold leaves are 'neath the snow,
and if we watch the maple
we know where winters go.

The maple tree is silent,
it is more still than still;
but leaves will soon be budding,
I know they will, they will.

## CONVERSATION: HOW FAR IS HEAVEN?

How far is it to you from here?
*How far do you think?*
Is it close?
*It's as far as you think.*
I am thinking of you.
*I am right here.*
Does it seem far away to you?
*Heaven can be very near.*
Is heaven in the mind?
*It's one of the rooms.*
One of the rooms is in me?
*When you remember me, I am right here.*
I think of you always.
*The mind is a big room. I am with you always.*
And I am always with you.
*It is true.*

## It's Never Over

God,
you woke with light the darkness,
you set the morning star,
now help us trust your nearness
when things seem far too far.

God,
you raise the trees from winter,
you birth the rising sun,
now give a new beginning
when things seem gone and done.

God,
you whispered to the sleeping,
then rolled the stone away,
now help us find direction
when we would lose the way.

God,
you started life within us,
a baby we would grow,
you said it's never over
and who but you could know.

## Conversation: An Autumn Walk

I wish you could see the color of the woods.
   *What is it you see?*
The way the trees are decorated. I notice it more since you left.
   *I can be with you when you see them. Tell me the trees*
   *and colors you like most.*
The red oak, and the yellow of the weeping willow.
   *How was the color before, in other years?*
I don't remember looking. I didn't think about seeing it with
someone as much as I do now. If only you could see what I see.
   *I can be close to you while you look, if you want someone you*
   *love to see it also.*
I do love you. That is why I am staying here for a while, just
looking.
   *You can't hurry when something is as beautiful as autumn*
   *colors . . . or rainbows.*
I did not see rainbows as much before. Now I want you to see
them with me.
   *Keep looking for rainbows. Enjoy the colors.*
You are so little, and you know the power of colors. I talk to you
about oaks and willows and rainbows.
   *Rainbow is a household word.*
I feel I am holding you in my arms. You are so little, yet you
know so much.
   *When you are tired from holding me, hold onto me. I am*
   *strong. I am more than one age, more than one size.*
The willow leaves are falling.
   *Show me the color again when it is spring.*

## Brand New Tree

We planted you a brand new tree;
the autumn leaves came falling down
all red and yellow, golden brown,
a place nearby for you to be.

We planted you a brand new tree;
the winter snow came dancing down
and birds came flying all around,
a place nearby for you to be.

We planted you a brand new tree;
the summer sun did warm the ground
and green, green leaves did soon abound,
a place nearby for you to be.

You planted us a brand new tree;
our seasons sleep inside the ground,
the wind, the leaves, our silent sound,
a place for us with you to be.

## CONVERSATION: ASHES TO ASHES

I'm thinking of the funeral.
 *I was there.*
It was hard to sing. We sang a song we like.
 *Music helps. I have heard you hum many times.*
We spoke the words: "If I walk through the valley of the shadow
of death, I will fear no evil."
 *Good pictures help us understand. That's why children color.*
We ran out of tears.
 *For now. Tears keep coming. They wash the sight.*
Someone said: "Earth to earth, ashes to ashes."
 *That's what seed needs to live. Earth.*
Ashes, dust, earth, under a new tree.
 *In April it will all be green. In October there will be the colors.*
The sun will make them glow.
 *You will feel it. We know about glowing in heaven.*
Heaven. Earth. Sometimes so far.
 *Sometimes so near each other. Two sides of one life.*
You are in our earth.
 *You are in our heaven. The tree will make you glad.*
You make the tree good.
 *It is like the tree of life.*

## You Have Come to Stay

We didn't leave you in the earth
that silent, silent day;
you came to us before your birth
and you have come to stay.

I am your father, you began,
I heard your heart inside
and now my heart beats fast in me,
there's nothing I can hide.

I am your mother with a feast,
it stayed inside my breast;
I never heard you cry for drink
and then for all the rest.

We are the ones who know you best,
in us you chose to stay;
then while we loved you most of all
you went so soon away.

## Conversation: Others

They tried to help.
   *Helping is hard.*
Sometimes too much, too loudly, with too many words.
   *It is not easy to know. It is often the first time for them.*
They cried.
   *They felt a loss. Tears come.*
Some were silent. They had no words.
   *There was too much to say. Words are not always easy to find.*
Some did not understand our silence. They had to talk.
   *They had to. That is how it is with some.*
Some were just there, with us. Close.
   *They heard what you could not say out loud.*
They remember us with cards and gifts.
   *They will not quit. They will not let go of you.*
Some remember you by name. They say your name with all the others.
   *We all have a right to a name, and a right to keep it.*
When they look a certain way, you are there.
   *It will always be so.*
You will not go away.
   *Never. Nor will you.*

## I Wonder Why

They see us seem so silent,
we sometimes cry and so they say:
you'll be alright,
you'll be alright.
I wonder why
so then we turn away.

They turn their tears away.
They feel the tears, the silence,
we always laughed and now they say:
oh please don't cry.
I wonder why
they turn their grief away.

They hear the breath of silence,
we always laughed and now they say:
now don't be sad,
now don't be sad,
I wonder why
and then they look away.

## Conversation: The Blanket

We saved some of your baby clothes. We had a special blanket to cover you.

*You tucked me in all those months. I was wrapped in you.*

The blanket is yours.

*It can be a hand-me-down.*

It has its own place.

*We all have things. But they are not just our own.*

It's in the family.

*I am in the family.*

It may never be used.

*We all have many gifts that will never be opened. There are so many.*

Some cry when I mention the blanket.

*They too have saved something they could not use.*

I want to put the quilt on you.

*Do it. Only you have to know.*

Will you feel it?

*You taught me to feel. I learned my feelings inside you.*

## LIKE FOG

Like fog at night there comes the blame
of them and then of me;
my eyes and voice are dim with shame
and only blame I see.

Like fog at night there comes the guilt
and who will know my heart
when fingers hold a brand-new quilt
yet dreams have come apart.

Like fog at night there comes the light,
a distant burning star,
and through the fog and tears of night
I know just where we are.


## CONVERSATION: SADNESS

Do you feel what I'm feeling?
    *Which feeling?*
My feeling of being so sad.
    *Sad feelings are part of other feelings.*
Sadness has other feelings touching it?
    *The feeling of want.*
I want you.
    *Wanting is universal.*

Do you want what I want?

*I want you, my mother, my father.*

Then you know how it feels to want you.

*I am what you want.*

What can I do with this feeling?

*Feel it. Want me.*

How did this feeling in me happen?

*You gave me months of life. I was in you.*

Now you are in my mind. I cannot get you off my mind.

*Hold me there, in your mind.*

In wanting you?

*That is how I began. You wanted me. We wanted each other.*
*I came.*

The time went so fast.

*We met.*

You are not sad?

*I was formed in love. I feel the love.*

The love we had?

*The love we will always have.*

Then you know the feeling of being sad.

*And wanting and having.*

## Love You So

How can you make us love you so
when we have barely met?
Inside where we could never see
we felt the life and love of thee.
Our eyes are very wet.

How can you make us love you so
when we have barely met?
Were you waiting since long time ago,
someone we now will always know?
Our eyes are very wet.

> *I came when you two loved me so,*
> *and there we first did meet;*
> *we'll meet again along a shore*
> *where life is long and love is more,*
> *to see what never eyes did see*
> *unless the eyes were wet.*

## Conversation: Change

Everything is changed. It's all different now.
>   *Nothing stays the same.*
It changed when you came and then went. I miss you so.
>   *How is it different now?*
I didn't miss you before.
>   *Now you know me. We know each other.*
You know me?
>   *There are ways to know someone, to be together.*
We are together. We are related.
>   *Being part of the gene pool is a big connection.*
I miss you. I imagine your voice.
>   *Voice is one way to be close. I lived inside you.*
We met in the big pool, and so it was the three of us.
>   *I was never alone. You were there.*
We felt you move. We played music. You turned somersaults;
we smiled.
>   *I swam.*
We laughed knowing you were there.
>   *I danced. I swam. I drank.*
You danced to our music.
>   *With you.*
Did you like the music?
>   *It is still with me.*
It's different now.
>   *What's inside doesn't disappear.*
Now it's different from how it ever was.
>   *Now it's forever.*

I am in you, you are in me.
    *We are more connected than ever.*
And in the future?
    *Forever and ever.*
Everything is changed.
    *Everything changes.*
There's a big difference.
    *We have made a difference to each other.*

## A Baby Whom I Know

As tiny seed in garden bed
I hold a child inside my head,
sometimes it blooms pure white, deep red,
a tiny baby in my head.

I found an oak to hold a swing
to fly my baby on the wing,
together we did laugh and sing;
beneath the oak we swing, we swing.

A baby I did come to know;
inside my mind the baby grows
as clouds keep coming, then they go.
There is a baby whom I know.

## Conversation: Private Pain

They are giving me books to read about you and me.
> *They love you.*

They are writing me cards I cannot read now.
> *They are writing their own feelings.*

And they are praying for me.
> *It is their medicine.*

They did not birth you as we did.
> *They want to understand their own hurt.*

I cannot read their words.
> *You have your own words to say and write.*

I am writing you.
> *Each person has words of their own.*

I do not tell them my words. I do not read them myself.
> *It is too soon.*

I will not read their words.
> *First you need to know your own words.*

They think of me when they write.
> *And of me. This is how they express their pain.*

The words are about us. They cannot help.
> *It is about them and us. They know me.*

Not as we know you.
> *It is their way to keep me alive.*

We will keep you alive, forever.
> *We all keep each other alive.*

I am closest to you.
> *And I will keep you alive.*

You are so little.
*A spirit has strength*
I am the one to keep you real.
*With the others.*
I birthed you. I am the mother.
*And there is my father. You both gave me this lifetime.*
We will keep you alive.
*We will all keep each other alive.*

## THE EYES I SEE

There are the people all around,
the air is full of loving sound,
some words I hear will grow with me
like seed inside the ground.

There are the looks inside the eyes
when silence dims the muted cries;
the eyes I see that stay with me,
those taken by surprise.

## Conversation: Longing

I should have prevented your leaving so soon.
> *What do you mean by leaving?*

I cannot see you.
> *What are you looking for?*

For you.
> *One can't see everything that is real.*

I wanted to see you grow as a child. At least for awhile.
> *Would awhile be long enough?*

You made me insatiable.
> *For what?*

For you, for knowing you.
> *What do you want to know?*

How we would have played.
> *How do you want to play? You choose the game.*

How we would have gone places.
> *Choose the place.*

How we would have laughed.
> *Let's laugh.*

We would have made music.
> *Choose the song.*

I wanted to have you for awhile, a long while.
> *You will have me for a long while. As long as there is time.*

I want to see you.
> *Take a look. What do you see?*

I want to be with you, very close.
> *How close?*

As close as we are, right now.
> *Listen. We are very close.*

## EVERYWHERE

When I had no tears to cry
you were there;
when I found no word to say
you were there;

When I too tried to take the blame
you were there;
when I wished myself to die
you were there;

When I found no place to hide
you were there.

You are there,
everywhere.

## Conversation: Guilt

I hate for you to see me this way.
>*What are you feeling now?*
Guilty.
>*You did me no harm.*
Do you forgive me?
>*If that is what you want, I forgive you.*
You're not angry?
>*You brought me into being.*
For only a little while.
>*It isn't over.*
Do you know how I feel?
>*I was in you all the time.*
Then you know.
>*You showed me all your feelings.*
They don't make you sad or angry.
>*You did me no harm.*

## Forgive Me

Why do I feel so guilty?
You know I thought of you each step I took,
each work I did;
everything was ready and now look.

I look, I look
into the time I took such care,
took you gladly, dearest, everywhere;
gathered clothes for you to wear,
never thought how long it took.

Now look, now look.
Forgive me, forgive me,
if I did any harm to thee;
forgive me, forgive me,
I pray thee, I pray thee.

> *You gave my soul a form,*
> *you kept me safe and warm,*
> *you did no wrong or harm;*
> *I have a life reborn.*

## Conversation: I Can't Pray

All my feelings keep me from praying.
> *These feelings are the prayer.*

There are too many feelings for words.
> *Praying doesn't need many words.*

My feelings keep repeating themselves.
> *Lots of songs repeat the same words, the same tunes.*

Do you have a prayer you repeat?
> *Prayers last longer when they have music with them.*

My feelings aren't making a song.
> *The music can come later.*

My feelings have different chords, different keys.
> *Every prayer gets its own score.*

My prayer needs a melody.
> *The tune is inside the feelings.*

Do you know the songs I want to sing?
> *Songs come from where I am.*

You know them by heart?
> *You cannot hide music from a living soul.*

Do you sing?
> *Souls sing. There will always be spirit choirs.*

Would you sing with me?
> *We can take turns.*

What will you sing?
> *I can sing what you feel.*

Do you know the tune?
> *When I hear you I will know the tune.*

What if it makes you cry?
> *I will let you hold me when we sing.*
Then what?
> *Then it's my turn; you can sing my song.*
Will I know it?
> *It will surprise you.*
Will I cry?
> *We will dance when we sing the song I want to sing.*

## HEAVEN IS YOUR HOME

I know that heaven is your place;
it's better than the sights we see,
your sights inside eternity,
and still I long for your embrace.

I know that heaven is your home;
there is no pain, there is no fear,
God wipes away your ev'ry tear
and still I feel I am your home.

Tears seem to flow and never stop.
Dear God of parents who must weep
help us to know what we must keep
so we on earth keep looking up.

## Conversation: Winter Life

You were born so still.
>*Something still is still at work.*

You didn't move.
>*You can't always see what moves.*

I couldn't feel the warmth.
>*Winter seems cold. But deep inside the earth is warm.*

You know about winter?
>*Life always has seasons. I came as winter.*

When will it be spring?
>*Here the River is flowing, the trees are green.*

It is a long winter here.
>*The sun can warm some winters in a night.*

That quickly?
>*Being warm comes from a little town.*

A town?
>*Bethlehem.*

You know about Bethlehem?
>*Some winters thaw in a night.*

What breaks the hard ice in winter?
>*Light.*

Where does your light come from?
>*From the beginning. It goes through Bethlehem.*

You can see it with your eyes?
>*We don't look just with our eyes.*

You have a good imagination?
>*We believe.*

## Moon Is Waning

Again the moon is waning,
and brighter now each star;
the Christmas bells are ringing.
I see what time we are.

Again the moon is waning,
the dark has swept the light
while moon mirrors the daytime
and we want sleep at night.

Again the moon is waning,
far brighter than each star;
Is that high place called heaven
where you and angels are?

## Conversation: Searching for the Center

You're quiet.

> *I thought you might be sleeping.*

It doesn't matter. You don't have to whisper for my sake.

> *But I must for mine. I am often still.*

For my sake?

> *More for mine.*

It's quiet in the center of the storm.

> *We all can see it first hand. Close your eyes. Be still.*

I am still. It is quiet inside the center.

> *One has to find the center.*

Where it is still.

> *It can take a while.*

Do you talk about peace and quiet?

> *It isn't necessary to talk about the silence.*

It can speak for itself.

> *Quiet has its own sound. Silence can be more powerful than the storm.*

You can't stay there all the time.

> *You can go there, to the center. That's what we're doing.*

We're going to the center for a while.

> *Everyone can find the silence in the center of the storm.*

## LOVE

Love is as a butterfly inside the summer sun,
it touches tips of blossoms
for the touching is the fun.

Love can be a tiny hand, the fingers holding mine;
it holds me by the fingertips
as does a climbing vine.

Love can be a footprint along the ocean shore,
two footprints in a single walk;
I wish there could be more.

Love can be the quiet in the center of a storm
when all around is tumbling
while you and I stay warm.

Love can be a long distance when all I want is you
to kiss as lips of tulips
will touch the morning dew.

## Conversation: Let-there-be

I've run out of words.
>*I know about words.*

You never spoke a word.
>*I know the Word, the One whose name is the Word.*

We wanted to teach you to count, to say the ABCs.
>*I know the Word.*

Is it the word *mama,* daddy?
>*I know the birthing Word.*

All words come from this word?
>*All our words. It's name: the Word.*

Is it a word we know?
>*It is the mother, the father of all words.*

Is it a noun?
>*All nouns, all verbs, begin in the Word.*

Whisper the word to me.
>*Let-there-be.*

That is the word?
>*Let-there-be.*

All words begin with Let-there-be?
>*Let-there-be birthed light and life.*

That was in the beginning.
>*And in our beginning. Let-there-be, and I was.*

Your life.
>*Our life.*

Let-there-be is the oldest word. The Word.
>*The Word became flesh and lived among us.*

You see the Word?
*I behold the glory of the Word.*
If I could only see the glory.
*Glory is too bright to see. We behold glory.*


## WHERE

Where is the field of souls unborn
where breath will choose nativity
to dance a life on earth
in birth?

Where is the field of souls unborn
where words of songs choose melodies
to dance new tunes on earth
in mirth?

Where is the field of souls unborn
where grace of God calls out a name
to take for life a birth
on earth?

Where is the field of souls unborn
where Let-there-be waits human form
to dance by heart on earth
a birth?

## CONVERSATION: THROUGH GOD

Can you see me?
> *We all see each other.*

You can see my face?
> *We see what we love.*

You see my face me because we're related.
> *I see you because you're in the direction of Alpha,*
> *the Beginning.*

When you face me, you see Alpha?
> *And when I face Alpha, I see you.*

Where is Alpha?
> *In you. When I look for Alpha, the Beginning, I see you.*

How do you see Alpha?
> *By believing.*

How do I see you?
> *When you see Alpha, you see me.*

Alpha is where you are.
> *Alpha is in me, between us.*

Then I can see you through Alpha.
> *Yes, we met in the Beginning.*

Is it only through the Beginning?
> *Only through Alpha. Before my beginning we did not see*
> *each other.*

Then the beginning is not past.
> *The Beginning is in us.*

Connecting us.
> *Uniting us as in the Beginning.*

## Always Here

Long before we knew you,
where were you?
You came to us brand-new
and still it seems you were always near,
always here.

Long before we knew you,
where were you?
You'll always be right here
and where we go you are always there,
anywhere.

How can you be so far and near,
so close, so far away,
all night and then all day?
How can you be anywhere and here,
everywhere?

## Conversation: Christmas

You went so soon. There was so little time.
*There are lots of parts to time.*
You went to heaven before we got started here.
*We are started. You are talking to me.*
I wanted to have days together, weeks, years.
*Pick a time. We can be together.*
Yesterday. We could have decorated the tree together.
*Was I there with you?*
I thought of you the whole time, with each straw decoration
I hung. You helped me put each one on the right twig.
*Would it have gone quicker if I had handed them to you?*
You would have been too little.
*What could I have done?*
You could have watched me, enjoyed each decoration.
*It was very cold outside by the tree.*
You felt very near. You seemed to be there.
*That is my special gift, that I could be there, being so little.*
You don't just seem little now.
*So you have me from the future, when I will be older.*
You aren't just one age to me now.
*That's how it is with time. We can borrow what we missed.*

## It's Christmas

It's Christmas,
the baby in the manger,
joy to the world, and I am filled with fear.

It's Christmas,
the baby is in danger,
peace upon earth, my soul is filled with tears.

It's Christmas,
the baby in the straw;
I see all tiny babies, my soul is filled with awe.

## Conversation: Where Is Laughter?

I do not laugh as often as before.
*Laughter will come.*
There are too many tears.
*Tears are sometimes near laughter.*
I cannot laugh about my feelings.
*A soul can laugh.*
Out loud?
*One can laugh quietly.*
Are you joyful?
*We praise, we sing, we give thanks.*
Your heart is glad?
*Filled with thanks.*
For what do you give thanks?
*For life.*
It was so short.
*My life is begun.*
We barely saw your life. It was hidden in me.
*It was created inside you. You both were my world, in which*
*I found life.*
Barely begun.
*I live.*
We wanted you in our family, in our house.
*I am in your family. I can show you others in the family.*
I mean our family.
*The family I know is our family.*
Do you know their names?
*Francis, Clara, Augustine, Maria, Sarah.*

Names of those who have gone. You know these names.
> *We all have names.*

Do you call each other by names?
> *You need the names. That is how you think of me, and of the others.*

When I say your name, I cry.
> *The name can start the tears, then the tears can be wiped away.*

## SOMETIMES

Sometimes I find a song hid in an April tree,
the wind makes leaves and branches
a summer melody.

Sometimes I find a song when apple orchards bloom,
the petals then descending
to dance away my gloom.

Sometimes I find a song tucked in a garden bed,
I buy one rose for you
and paint the music red.

Sometimes I find a song hid in the thought of you,
together we go singing
of words we know are true.

Sometimes I find a song inside a baby cry,
I cannot sing the melody,
you know the reason why.

## Conversation: Souls in Heaven

Did they know you when you came?
 *They did not forget me.*
They knew you before?
 *I had just left.*
So they still knew you.
 *We all know each other.*
Do I know them?
 *You will.*
How will I know them?
 *You will remember them.*
By their names?
 *In lots of ways.*
The way I remember you.
 *Not just by my name.*

# I Heard a Voice

I heard a voice that sounded just like you,
whose voice I never heard;
it come from deep inside the wood,
the chirping of a bird.

I heard a voice that sounded just like you,
it sounded just like you,
it came from deep inside the wood
beneath the morning dew.

I heard a voice that sounded just like you,
whose voice was never spoke;
it came from deep inside the wood,
the silent, silent oak.

## Conversation: Sledding

I wanted to go sledding with you.
*Where did you want to ride? Where is the hill?*
The one where I rode before you. Near the maple tree we
planted for you.
*When would we ride?*
When you were older.
*Why do you want this ride?*
The thrill for you. For me, sharing the thrill of the swiftness
with a child.
*What is this feeling like?*
Like when I was young. I can feel that time.
*When did you feel it last?*
I feel it now, looking north at the hillside. I can feel you clinging
to me.
*Is it dangerous?*
Perhaps for me. Not for you.
*You feel the ride?*
I see us coming through the snow, the wind against our faces;
we're screaming with laughter.
*Both of us.*
You riding on me, clinging as I did to my father.
*How fast are we going?*
As fast as back then, when I loved to slide this hill.
*You don't love it now?*
With you I do.
*Come. Let's go again.*

## WINTER SLIDE

I hoped we'd take a winter slide,
cold wind upon the face;
a door then opened very wide
and you went to the other side
somewhere beyond this place.

I thought we'd take a wintry slide,
you went from us so soon,
you walked across a river wide
to live inside the other side
with angels 'round your room.

> *You'll come into this place so wide*
> *to look where I now see,*
> *to see beyond and far inside;*
> *just close your eyes, be at my side*
> *and there you'll walk with me.*

## Conversation: Do You Worry?

Do you worry?
>*God keeps watch.*

Where did you learn that?
>*We believe God keeps watch.*

Who talks about it with you?
>*We don't talk about it; it's the way it is.*

What's it like when God keeps watch?
>*Being held, being known, being safe.*

You know these feelings?
>*It's how God keeps watch.*

We wanted to watch over you.
>*You do; when God keeps watch, you keep watch.*

If God keeps watch what do we do?
>*Keep watch with God.*

Over each other?
>*And ourselves. God keeps watch over me, over you.*

I wake at night wanting to watch over you.
>*God keeps watch.*

What am I to do?
>*Go to sleep. God keeps watch over me and you.*

Don't we have anything to do?
>*To let God keep watch. That is enough.*

In the night?
>*Know that God does it, to me, to you.*

What else can I do in the night?
>*Sleep.*

## A Wind Blows

A wind blows down a summer nest,
the oriole stands by
to wait till wind and storm are past
and does not reason why.

A wind blows down a summer nest,
once more they build the nest,
the oriole sings on the wing
and finds what feels the best.

A wind blows down a brand new nest,
I hear a melody,
the oriole flies back and forth
to build what now will be.

## Conversation: Colors

We had a box of crayons just for you.
>*How many colors?*

Forty-eight in one box. You never got to see them.
>*There are many colors here. More than forty-eight.*

Can you count to forty-eight?
>*We don't count one by one. There are too many.*

Too many numbers for counting?
>*Too many colors to count. We stand in awe.*

Of colors?
>*Of beauty.*

It's beautiful?
>*Yes. It's more than all the colors. More bright and pastel
>and sparkling.*

Colors brighter than the sun?
>*Brighter than all suns, all moons, and all stars.*

The Book tells of jasper and jewels, rubies and diamonds.
>*That's some of the beauty.*

And the River.
>*The River of Life.*

Clear blue water.
>*More than water. A river of peace and joy.*

Waves and white caps?
>*Clapping their hands. Singing with the colors.*

Rising and falling?
>*Dancing with the colors. Colors in ecstasy.*

Do you call it color? Do you call it beauty?
>*We call it light.*

The colors and beauty of light.
*The rhythms and the sounds of light waves.*
You know about light waves and sound waves?
*Here light and song and life are one.*

## AN OLIVE BRANCH

God,
you saved the ark inside the sea,
there was no room to row,
now save the hurt of humankind
inside your own rainbow.

God,
the waves are long, the billows high,
the storm will hide the light,
so guide us through this storm we know
that hides you in plain sight.

God,
a storm will rock the sea and roar,
a dove then flies the rain
and brings an olive branch of peace
to still our human pain.

## Conversation: Alright

It's hard.
>    *What is hard?*
Believing that it's alright.
>    *What's alright?*
Everything. You. Me. Us.
>    *It's alright with me.*
What's alright?
>    *Where I am, everything is alright.*
Where is everything alright?
>    *Far inside, that's where alright is with me. Deep inside.*
Deep inside can be alright? You have a place like that?
>    *Souls have peace deep inside and all around.*
Peace stays there?
>    *It grows, it spreads. It glows, like glory.*
You glow?
>    *All souls have glory.*
Then it's alright with you?
>    *The glory won't fade, not here.*
You mean where you are, peace won't go away.
>    *Peace and light can't end. In me. In you. Things that deep and bright won't stop.*
I felt peace in me when we first knew of you. Nothing will take its place.
>    *Things don't have to replace each other.*

You take up so much room in me.
> *There's lots of room in us, around us. There's a lot of space*
> *where I am. I know the space in you.*

You were with us, inside for many days. You filled up this space
in me.
> *What was in that space before?*

Feelings, thoughts, of what we wanted.
> *Then I came into that space in you.*

You filled the space. You are always on my mind, on our minds.
> *That's the way it still is. It is alright.*

## I STAND IN AWE

Dear God,
the world seemed once so small,
I held it inside me,
then in a moment I did find
the world we have is inside Thee;
in tears I stand in awe.

Dear God,
the world seemed once so small,
a baby inside me,
then in one moment I did find
there is a world in Thee;
in tears I stand in awe.

## CONVERSATION: THE RIVER

Have you been to the river?
>*It runs down Main Street.*

The river?
>*The River of Life.*

Is it clear?
>*We swim in it.*

You know how to swim?
>*We learn it in our mothers.*

So you know the River.
>*It's all one water, one River, one Life.*

We were going to teach you to swim and climb.
>*There is the Tree of Life.*

Beside the River?
>*On both sides. It bears fruit.*

You eat the fruit?
>*Here we do. It's always in season.*

Where does the River begin?
>*You know, in the Beginning.*

It's the same River?
>*It's all one water. One Tree. One Life.*

Where does the River end?
>*It keeps going on and on.*

## There Is a River

There is a river deep inside
I never knew before,
it has a spring that never quits,
I wipe my tears and soon there come some more, some more.

There is river deep inside
I did not know it there,
when you were born I found it first
and now it springs from everywhere, from everywhere.

There is a river deep inside,
a river very deep;
so many times I meet you, dear,
I meet you in the river when I weep, when I weep.

## Conversation: Reading

We could have read books together.
>    *What book do you like?*
I would have read *The Chronicles of Narnia* with you.
>    *You can read it now.*
I am. I started just after you left.
>    *Did I leave?*
After you went to heaven.
>    *The book about the Lion.*
The miracles behind the doors, inside closets, in far spaces.
>    *Heavenly spaces and sounds.*
I am reading as though you are with me.
>    *Am I old enough for* Narnia *stories?*
You seem old enough. We talk about all kinds of things.
>    *So you are reading with me and talking to me.*
I wonder how it is there, really. How it is behind the doors, in
the attic closets.
>    *How does* Narnia *seem to you this time?*
It's different this time. Then I read it alone. Now we're reading it
with each other.
>    *Are you reading out loud?*
Almost out loud. As though you can hear me.
>    *Pretending?*
Not pretending. The reading is more real than the first time.
We're looking at everything from here and from there.
>    *Me and you.*

From now and then, from earth and from heaven.
    *How does it read now?*
Higher, deeper, farther, wider.
    *Nearer?*
It's all nearer.
    *We are near?*
Very near each other.

# I See the Sights

I see the sights you never saw,
the beauty of this season;
I cry where I once felt in awe,
I know, I know the reason.

I hear the sounds you never learned,
the melodies, the tunes,
the larks, the robins in the spring,
the haunting mourning loons.

I hope you hear these things I hear
and see what I now see
and feel the thoughts I know by heart
and hold inside of me.

I know the stories often read,
I've heard it often told
that you can see far more than we
and nothing there is old.

One wish that comes most ev'ry day
is that you feel the awe
that brings quick tears into my eyes
of sights I wish you saw.

## Conversation: Music

You would have been in a choir soon.
> *Every soul sings.*

You sing?
> *Soul music.*

Are you in a children's choir?
> *All sing at once.*

In different choirs?
> *It's one space.*

Aren't the rooms divided?
> *Space overlaps.*

The choirs hear each other?
> *Harmonize.*

You don't have rows and sections?
> *We sing from inside, from the center.*

Different anthems?
> *One song, one choir, one director.*

Standing on a high podium?
> *Directing from the center.*

In the middle of everyone?
> *In the middle of each soul.*

At the same time?
> *There's only one time. Now is forever.*

Is there an audience?
> *All sing and all hear.*

Do I know the songs you know?
> *All music is born here. All songs have the same refrain.*

Then we all join in the chorus.
> *All know the chorus, the word: Amen.*

The refrain is one word?
>*Amen. That is the chorus: Amen.*

You hear when I sing Amen.
>*We all sing Amen at once.*

Could we ever sing a duet?
>*We always do.*

## I Sing a Song

I sing a song of rocking, rocking
you in my rocking chair,
and while we're rocking, rocking, rocking,
I wonder why and where.

I sing a song of holding, holding
you close against my breast,
and while I'm holding, holding, holding,
you give my soul a rest.

I sing a song of weeping, weeping,
I hear you sound asleep,
and while I'm weeping, weeping, weeping,
two angels watch do keep.

I sing a song of walking, walking,
your footprints in the sand,
and while I'm walking, walking, walking,
we two walk hand in hand.

## Conversation: Your Birthday

It's your birthday. We should celebrate.
  *What do you want to do?*
So many things. And nothing.
  *Mention something you want to do.*
Give you flowers.
  *Flowers show a lot of feeling. A bouquet?*
A plant. One that puts down roots, that grows and blooms.
  *Alive.*
That's what I want for your birthday.
  *Where will you plant it?*
Where I can see it, watch it bud and blossom.
  *What about the winter?*
We will cover it to keep it safe. When the cold is gone we will
see it break through the earth, green again.
  *Like a birth.*
Rebirth. We will give you a perennial.
  *I also like annuals.*
They die.
  *They leave behind seeds. In the spring, they sprout, then bloom.*
Easter comes in the spring.
  *That's when violets are in full bloom.*
We don't buy violets. They are always here.
  *Then violets will do for my birthday. They are always there.*
They live through winter. And they seed.
  *They are tiny and tender.*
We know the feeling, tiny and tender.

# I Am Here

If you were here for birthdays;
we'd show you candle lights,
we'd give you teddy bears galore,
we'd gladly buy the candy store,
and still,
we know you see all these and more
and all the colors of the lights;
we sing
and you hear angels on the wing.

## Conversation: Walking

If you had lived, you'd be walking.
>*I am alive.*

Here we walk, we run. Your mother is a runner.
Your father bikes.
>*We know. We cheer you on. But here we go faster than walking.*

Do you climb mountains?
>*We ascend and descend.*

Do you go far?
>*Distance isn't the same here.*

But how far are you?
>*Close.*

Like miles or inches?
>*We don't measure distance. We are not apart.*

If you're out of breath, you wait for each other?
>*We see places from all sides here.*

How does it really work?
>*You have to be here to know how it works.*

Can't you tell me?
>*You will see. You will.*

# I Know

You never took a step.
*I know.*
You never walked the winter hill,
you did not hear our whippoorwill,
you left a footprint in the snow.
*I know.*

You never took a step.
*I know.*
You did not see the tulips bloom,
you did not watch the stars or moon,
you left a footprint here below.
*I know.*

You never took a step.
*I know.*
You never slept against my breast,
you never saw the east or west,
you leave a footprint where I go.
*I know.*

## Conversation: Meeting Place

We have a place we go to be near you.

> *Some have a stone, a rock, a lake. You have a tree.*

We planted it that same week. A memorial. We go there; there's a bench.

> *I know about special places. I was in you. You both heard my heart.*

We both knew you were there. It was our place to be with you.

> *Now you have the maple tree.*

Not only there. Lots of places remind us of you.

> *So it is with places. They are sacred. Each place is like being home.*

But not all places seem so special.

> *Here all space is holy. All are in God.*

You talk that way in heaven?

> *That's how it is, here and there, the same. We are all in God. We are inside the circle.*

Then you have a universe.

> *The universe is also in God. The planets, the maple tree, you, me.*

We all fit?

> *It's one family. One dust, one earth, one breath, one spirit, one life.*

You breathe?

> *Spirit is breath. It's life.*

You consider yourself living?

> *We are all in God's life. That is the life we have. There is one breath, one life.*

Does it stop? Do you hear when life quits?

> *Life doesn't end. Your spirit will breathe.*

## WE MEET

A leaf comes falling in the wind,
it's one more autumn time;
I kneel and take the broken bread,
it's more than bread and wine.

Inside the holy sacrament
I broke the bread and cried,
then visited the place you went
to kneel down by your side.

Ev'ry place I ever go
I find a moment sweet
and see the things I cannot know
and there with you we meet.

## Conversation: Work

I was looking forward to your future.
*The future is my present.*
I was looking forward to tomorrow and all the years of your life.
*This is my life.*
I had hope for your life's work. I had a work in mind for you.
*I am at work.*
You won't miss going to school? Having a job, running
a company?
*I am in a company.*
Your company is secure?
*I'm in a company of angels.*
What do you do?
*What I am doing in you, and in others.*
Who knows about you?
*You know. Others. People in many lands.*
So you have work to do.
*There is enough to do, and it is good.*
Something for which you will be remembered?
*For which I am needed.*
A work you'll be known for?
*Loved.*
You are young for all this.
*We do what we do best.*
It is your gift?
*It is all I need to give.*
You like your work?
*I was made for this place and time.*

Are you sure?
*We are all certain.*
You are in the right place.
*I'm in the right place at the right time.*
You are at peace.
*It is a perfect fit.*
Did you volunteer?
*I was chosen.*


# IF

If I were a shepherd I'd want you as my lamb,
I'd walk you by my side,
I'd take you for a ride,
I'd carry you with pride;
I'd be the shepherd, you the lamb.

If I were a mountain I'd make you the top,
we'd look all around,
look down to the ground,
you'd hear my heart pound;
I'd be a mountain, you the top.

If I had a kingdom I'd give you my throne,
you'd sit at my right,
I'd give you my light,
I'd show you pure delight.
There is a kingdom; you are near the throne.

## Conversation: Another Soul

A friend is dying. He lived ninety-six years.
*Some come sooner.*
Look for him. I can tell him you'll be waiting.
*It's not like waiting here. We are expecting him.*
Then you know about his being sick.
*Everybody comes. We expect everyone.*
You look forward to us coming?
*It is always happening. We come and go.*
Do you miss them when they leave?
*They don't really leave. They return. Everyone comes here.*
His family is waiting for him to go. They have been anxious for
two months.
*We are not anxious. All go and come. There is no other way.*
You are resigned to it?
*It is a gift to us. We have a turn.*
To be on earth.
*And here. To live.*
But you did not live.
*My life in you is not finished.*
We count you as a member of the family. We mention your name.
*It is not possible for me to leave you. You conceived me.*
We still want you. We hold you.
*I hold you. I am rooted in you, and you in me.*
We were one.
*We are one.*
My friend is coming.
*You are also.*

## Turtle Dove

Each turtle dove so quiet
steps through the wintry snow
to find a spread of dinner
until the sunsets go.

How careful is their walk
to find their feast of food,
their silence is a prayer.
Oh winter-time, be good.

Two turtle doves on tiptoe,
the snow is holy ground;
I hear it in their cooing,
they hear their hallowed sound.

Two turtle doves are going
where angels also tread;
the winter sun is setting
and soon they find their bed.

## Conversation: Time

The years go by.

> *They are always here. We don't call them years. We call them now.*

What time is it there? Do you have morning and night?

> *We have them all at once. It is always dark and light. It is*
> *always morning and sunset. Just as on the earth.*

We can't be two places at once. We don't see sunset and sunrise
at the same time.

> *When we are in the presence of God, it is always all the time.*

You don't have yesterday and tomorrow?

> *We are always in the presence of God, in the present tense.*

Then you have no clocks ticking, no stop watches.

> *We don't break time down that way.*

Then you don't count days and hours.

> *Count the moments. Who can count them all?*

We are to count our blessings, sometimes one by one.

> *They are all one. It is one blessing. That's what we live in,*
> *the one blessing.*

It isn't something you count?

> *It's greater than a number. Blessing surrounds us. We live inside it.*

Blessing is always there?

> *Blessing does not come and go.*

Then you don't look forward to, and wish, and want, and wait for?

> *We are in the presence of God. There is no greater want for us.*
> *We have the present.*

What about the future?
    *It is always coming to us.*
And the past?
    *The past is this talk we are having.*
It's not over.
    *The past is here, now.*

## INSIDE YOURSELF AND ME

Another birthday come and gone;
I watched you blow the candles
and make a wish with me,
the candles all went out,
not one was left;
the wish I make with you
is now inside of me.

What would I be without this way
of birthdays just for you,
that come so silently each year,
once more you blowing candles.
You know the years I see:
I feel a silent, silent tear
of pride inside yourself and me.

## CONVERSATION: THE RACE

You went so fast.
*I ran the race.*
It's taking me a lot longer. Did you finish?
*I crossed the line. I went all the way.*
The finishing line? You crossed the end?
*The line is not the end.*
Was it too fast? Were you exhausted?
*It seemed just right. It's all in how you see it.*
You see?
*We see.*
Clearly?
*Face to face. That's the way. Just as you live face to face.*
That's how I want to see you, face to face.
*When you cross the line, that's how we see: face to face.*
If you ran the race who were you running against?
*Myself. Each one runs that way. Against yourself.*
Then you win.
*Then you don't have to lose the race. You win.*
No regrets?
*Not when you see what face to face looks like. We give thanks.*
How long did it take?
*We don't measure in minutes or miles. There is no stop watch.*
Where is the end?
*We call it a new beginning.*

## Long Years

Long years are now behind me,
I've seen the stars and moon,
I've walked among the gardens;
you came, you left so soon.

I have long years behind me
and you had just begun,
I'd trade all my tomorrows
if you could feel the sun.

> *Where I am is no darkness,*
> *it's brighter than the sun,*
> *here is the clearest river;*
> *I see it on the run.*

> *We know of no tomorrows,*
> *we have no yesteryear,*
> *we feel no pain or sorrow*
> *for love has dimmed all fear.*

## CONVERSATION: MEETING AGAIN

When I come will you be there?
*I am here. I came, I know the way.*
Will I know how to find you?
*You will know the way. It's not like a road.*
Is it a door?
*It's the Way.*
Is someone in charge of the way?
*The Way.*
That's the name of the road?
*It's the name of the One who is the Way.*
You will be at the other side?
*It's not called the other side.*
Does it have a name?
*The Way.*
Is it a wide way or a long way?
*It is The Way; it changes the way we are, here and there.*
It's not like a highway or pathway.
*It changes the way we are, inside.*
The way we feel?
*And the way we think, and hear, and speak.*
The way we cry?
*And the way we laugh.*
It is the way things will be.
*It is the way we become.*
The way it could be?
*The way it is. It is the way it is.*

The way things will turn out?
*I mean the way it is now.*
You know that Way.
*It is the one Way, the only Way. The Way it is.*

## TODAY I DREAMED

Today I dreamt I let you go
as if you were a kite;
I let it go and go and go
until it flew out of sight.

Today I dreamed I let you go
as though I flew a kite;
I let it go and go and go,
it disappeared into the night.

Today I dreamed I let you go
as I once flew a kite;
I know that you did go and go
to fly into the brightest light.

Today I dreamed that I did go
as I once flew a kite,
and when I fly and go and go
I meet you in the flight.

# HELPFUL RESOURCES FOR THOSE WHO GRIEVE

## BOOKS

Gamino, Louis A., and Ann Taylor Cooney. *When Your Baby Dies Through Miscarriage or Stillbirth.* Hope and Healing Series. Minneapolis: Augsburg Books, 2002.

Hayford, Jack. *I'll Hold You in Heaven: Healing and Hope for the Parent Who Has Lost a Child Through Miscarriage, Stillbirth, Abortion or Early Infant Death.* Ventura, Calif.: Gospel Light Publications, 2003.

Smith, Harold Ivan. *Grievers Ask: Answers to Questions about Death and Loss.* Minneapolis: Augsburg Books, 2004.

Vredeveldt, Pam. *Empty Arms: Hope and Support for Those Who Have Suffered a Miscarriage, Stillbirth or Tubal Pregnancy.* Sisters, Ore.: Multnomah Publishers, 2001.

Westberg, Granger E. *Good Grief: A Faith-Based Guide to Understanding and Healing.* Minneapolis: Augsburg Books, 1971.

Wunnenberg, Kathe. *Grieving the Child I Never Knew.* Grand Rapids, Mich.: Zondervan, 2001.

## INTERNET SITES

Centering Corporation
*A non-profit organization dedicated to providing education and resources for the bereaved*
www.centeringcorp.com

The Compassionate Friends
*Guiding families toward the positive resolution of grief following the death of a child of any age and providing information to help others be supportive*
www.compassionatefriends.org

SHARE Pregnancy and Infant Loss Support, Inc.
*Providing support following the death of a baby through miscarriage, stillbirth or newborn death*
www.nationalshareoffice.com